INDIAN PRAIRIE PUBLIC LIBRARY
401 Plainfield Road
Darien, IL 60561

W9-ABU-936

AUG 1 9 2019

ROCKS, STICKS, AND THE FOREST FLOOR

By
Robin Twiddy

KidHaven
PUBLISHING

FOREST EXPLORER

Published in 2019 by KidHaven Publishing, an Imprint of Greenhaven Publishing, LLC
353 3rd Avenue, Suite 255, New York, NY 10010

© 2019 Booklife Publishing

This edition is published by arrangement with Booklife Publishing.

All rights reserved. No part of this book may be reproduced in any form
without permission in writing from the publisher, except by a reviewer.

Written by: Robin Twiddy
Edited by: Kirsty Holmes
Designed by: Gareth Liddington

Cataloging-in-Publication Data

Names: Twiddy, Robin.
Title: Rocks, sticks, and the forest floor / Robin Twiddy.
Description: New York : KidHaven Publishing, 2019. | Series: Forest explorer | Includes glossary and index.
Identifiers: ISBN 9781534528673 (pbk.) | ISBN 9781534528697 (library bound) | ISBN 9781534528680 (6 pack) |
ISBN 9781534528703 (ebook)
Subjects: LCSH: Forest ecology--Juvenile literature.
Classification: LCC QH541.5.F6 T963 2019 | DDC 577.3--dc23

Printed in the United States of America

CPSIA compliance information: Batch #BW19KL: For further information contact Greenhaven Publishing LLC, New York, New York at 1-844-317-7404.

Photocredits: All images are courtesy of Shutterstock.com.

Cover – Fotofermer, hddigital, valzan, EtiAmmos, vvoe, Nature energy, Nik Merkulov, kaprik, 1 – LedyX, 2 – Songquan Deng, 3 – JIANG HONGYAN,
4 – DAVE ALLEN PHOTOGRAPHY, VP Photo Studio, 5 – Nataliia K, Palo_ok, Gerrardkop, StudioSmart, 6 – katharinemolloy, valzan, 7 – EduardSV, 8 –
benjaminec, 9 – rogelson, 10 – Anna Kubczak, 11 – Nella, November27, 12 – Raffaella Galvani, nito, 14 – oliveromg, 15 – Jody Ann,
Vitalart, 16 – Mick Comien, 17 – Jack Hong, nadezhda F, 18 – EvgeniiAnd, 19 – Africa Studio, 20 – Vadim Chugaev, Chris Ison, Silver Spiral Arts, 21 –
Monkey Business Images, 22 – saam3rd, MyraMyra, Golden Shrimp, Egor Shilov, 23 – iko, Piotr Krzeslak.

Images are courtesy of Shutterstock.com. With thanks to Getty Images, Thinkstock Photo and iStockphoto.

All facts, statistics, web addresses and URLs in this book were verified as valid and accurate at time of writing.
No responsibility for any changes to external websites or references can be accepted by either the author or publisher.

CONTENTS

Words that look like **this** can be found in the glossary on page 24.

LET'S EXPLORE

WELCOME, FOREST EXPLORER!

Today we will be looking for sticks and rocks in the forest. You might be surprised by how exciting they can be!

4

GRAB YOUR EQUIPMENT

A budding forest explorer will need:

Camera

Magnifying Glass

Notebook

Boots

STICKS AND ROCKS

When exploring the forest you will probably come across lots of sticks and rocks. Each rock and each stick could be a whole mini **ecosystem** of its own!

If you are looking for interesting sticks and rocks, keep an eye on the ground.

Lots of animals make their homes with sticks and rocks, so be careful not to disturb them.

TYPES OF ROCKS

What color rocks can you find in the forest?

Rocks can be big or small, and can come in all sorts of shapes. Pebbles, stones, and boulders are all rocks. Keep an eye out for interesting ones.

In some forests you can find caves that are made out of rock. Caves can be dark, and some are not safe to explore. Make sure an adult goes with you.

!

SOMETIMES ANIMALS MIGHT BE LIVING OR HIDING IN CAVES. BE AWARE!

ROCK HABITATS

If you lift a rock up, you will find lots of insects living there. These insects like damp, dark places.

This wasp nest has been built in these rocks where it's **protected**.

Make sure you put any big rocks back, as they might be an animal's home.

Plants and **fungi** can grow on and around rocks. Rocks can be a very important part of the forest. They are **habitats** for insects, animals, and plants.

FUN WITH ROCKS

You can paint whatever you like on a stone – how about a funny face?

If you find some nice small rocks that fit in the palm of your hand, you could take one home and paint a picture on it.

If there is water in the forest, collect small, flat stones. See how many times you can skip a flat stone on the surface of the water.

TYPES OF STICKS

Sticks are really fun. They come in lots of very interesting shapes. Depending on what kinds of trees are in the forest, you will find different sticks.

BEAVERS USE
STICKS TO
BUILD DAMS
IN STREAMS.

Very big sticks are called logs; these are the branches of trees. Very small sticks are called twigs. Birds use twigs to make their nests.

STICK HABITATS

Use a magnifying glass to get a closer look!

Logs can be home to insects, mice, mushrooms, and plants. If you are looking for life in the forest, look closely at a log!

You might notice that some sticks are softer and easier to break. This is because they are rotting. Rotting sticks are good for the soil.

STICK INSECTS ARE CAMOUFLAGED TO LOOK LIKE SMALL STICKS.

FUN WITH STICKS

If you can find lots of strong sticks, you can build an explorer's den! You can also use a long stick as a walking stick.

Maybe you can plan where to explore next in your den!

Can you match the sticks you find in the forest with the trees they came from? Look to see if there is anything special about the bark or leaves.

Make a trail for your friends to follow through the forest with arrows made from sticks. Maybe it will lead to your den!

NATURE RESERVES

Some forests are protected. This means that you shouldn't take anything away from the forest, including sticks and rocks.

Check with an adult if it is OK for you to take a stick or rock home with you.

KEEPING NOTES

When you do find interesting rocks and sticks while exploring, it is important to keep careful notes. This way you will be able to **identify** them later.

Rock: Stone
Size: Medium
Color: Brown/Green

Wood: Willow
Size: 18–20cm
Color: Light Brown
Features: Y-Shape

Compare your notes with your friends'. See if they have found anything different.

GLOSSARY

aware	being alert and taking notice
camouflaged	when an animal is hard to see because it is the same color as its habitat
compare	to look at what is the same and what is different
ecosystem	a community of living things and the environment they live in
fungi	a type of life similar to plants but does not create food from sunlight – mushrooms, yeast, and molds are fungi
habitats	natural environments in which animals or plants live
identify	spot or recognize
protected	kept safe

INDEX